Sadie-Lynn is the light at the center of our world. She is thoughtful, joyful, and deeply in tune with the world around her. Though she doesn't speak with words, she communicates in ways that move us every single day. Her mom, Erechia, is her fiercest advocate and gentle guide – the heart behind every word in this book.

For Sadie's mom,
Erechia — your love
is endless.

For her dad, Jacob—
your strength is unwavering.

For her sister, Emma—
your laughter lights the way.

Hi. My name
is Sadie.

I don't use
words
to talk,
but
I listen
all the
time.

I hear more than just the words you say.

I hear voices.
I hear music.
I hear laughter.

I hear when someone is kind.

I CAN HEAR WHEN
SOMEONE IS NOT.

I hear you when you laugh.

I hear you when
you help me
with something new.

I hear you when
you believe in me.

I hear you when
we dance together.

I hear you even when
I am not looking at you.

I may not answer with words,
but I answer with my face,
my body and my heart.

Sometimes I flap when I'm excited.

Sometimes I cover my ears when it's too loud.

That's just me being
me in my own way.

You don't have to guess what I'm thinking.
You just have to see me, listen back,
and be patient.

Talk to me like anyone else.
Read with me.
Laugh with me.
Sit with me.

I hear you ...
because you listen to me, too.

Sensory-Friendly Tips

Keep environments calm and positive.

Give an extra moment for processing.

Model clear language and kind actions.

Provide options for breaks when it's overwhelming.

I hear you, even when the world is quiet.
Because your presence speaks louder than words.
And one day, my love, the world will listen too.
Love always,
Momma